Strawbery Banke and Monhegan Island

# THE SHAPE OF COLOR

Strawbery Banke and Monhegan Island

# THE SHAPE OF COLOR

## The paintings of Carol Aronson-Shore

Essays by Kimberly Alexander, Ph.D., and Mara Witzling, Ph.D.

Foreword by Robert Flynn Johnson

MUSEUM *of* ART
UNIVERSITY *of* NEW HAMPSHIRE

Blue Tree
PORTSMOUTH

First published in the United States in 2010
by Blue Tree, LLC
P.O. Box 148
Portsmouth, NH 03802

37 10 1

Front cover: *Morning Tree Shadows Behind the Yeaton-Walsh House*, oil on canvas, 30 x 30 in.
Back cover: *Lighthouse Museum Dory*, oil on canvas, 20 x 24 in.
Half-title page: *Groceries at Strawbery Banke*, oil on canvas, 12 x 24 in.
Frontispiece: *Signs at Strawbery Banke: Pottery and The Banks Gallery*, oil on canvas, 16 x 20 in.

This book is published in conjunction with the exhibition *The Shape of Color* held at the Museum of Art, University of New Hampshire.

For a complete viewing of works go to www.carolaronsonshore.com.

Printed in Hong Kong.

First edition, October 2010.

ISBN-13: 978-0-9792014-3-1
ISBN-10: 0-9792014-3-8

For customer service, orders, and book projects:
Local: 603.436.0831
Toll-Free: 866.852.5357
E-mail: sales@TheBlueTree.com

www.TheBlueTree.com

Blue Tree
A BOUTIQUE PUBLISHING FIRM

# PREFACE

Carol Aronson-Shore employs poetic effects of light, color, and composition to coax magical and mysterious moments out of our daily world. The Museum of Art, University of New Hampshire is pleased to be a partner with Jamie LaFleur of The Banks Gallery, Portsmouth, New Hampshire, and Brian Smestad of Blue Tree in this publication honoring Carol's luminous

*Strawbery Banke House in Fall*, gouache on paper, 5½ x 6 in. Private collection.

art career. A professor of painting and drawing at the University of New Hampshire from 1980 to 1999, Carol was named professor emeritus upon her retirement.

Carol has continued to pursue her muse through her evocative landscapes and seascapes. Her compositions are assured and assuring in their light and color relationships. Her professional success is amply demonstrated by the fact that she has exhibited, and is included in private and corporate collections, across the nation—including the permanent collection of the White House. The two essayists featured in the following pages will elaborate emphatically on Carol's artistic achievements.

The Museum of Art, University of New Hampshire has been pleased to host exhibitions of Carol's work over the years, in group shows as well as solo, and the one-person exhibition that is timed to coincide with the release of this book, in the fall of 2010, promises to be her most extensive. It should be noted that along with her artistic talent, Carol has demonstrated great generosity of spirit, as she has favored our permanent collection with gifts of artwork by her hand.

The University of New Hampshire is proud to participate in acclaiming the work and acknowledging the productive career that generated, in part at least, from the studios of this university, a vision dispersed through the artist/teacher and shared with her students over the course of her inspirational years on the art faculty. Kudos to Carol.

W. Weston LaFountain
Director
Museum of Art, University of New Hampshire

*Strawbery Banke Houses on Atkinson Street*, oil on canvas, 14 x 18 in.

# FOREWORD

*I carry my landscapes around with me.*

Joan Mitchell[1]

Emil Zola correctly observed that art was a corner of nature seen through a temperament. Sadly, today, in our postmodern world, art is defined and dominated by words (oh so many words!) with equally forceful denigration of artistic technique (a typical put-down these days is to condescendingly remark to an artist displaying solid draftsmanship or composition that their work displays "craft"). What is lost in our post-Duchampian era of effortless verbalized profundity is that art should, must, be a balance of ideas and execution. Ideas without the substance of a forcefully delineated composition are simple blather. In turn, however, virtuoso replication of reality without originality and inventiveness of idea is merely a demonstration of technical dexterity but is not true art. As James McNeill Whistler wrote, "The imitator is a poor kind of creature. If the man who paints only the tree, or flowers or other surface he sees before him were an artist, the king of artists would be the photographer. It is for the artist to do something beyond this."[2]

The strikingly personal landscape paintings of Carol Aronson-Shore are the successful transformation of her perception of nature and place through her mood and temperament into a decidedly subjective distillation of locations. Reference to specific geography is blessedly absent, replaced, in turn, by capturing the generalized essence of a locale through light, color, and form. The West Coast artist Wayne Thiebaud, whom Aronson-Shore admires, has also accomplished this over the years. Enamored of the flat planes of the Sacramento delta and the verticality of the hills of San Francisco, Thiebaud has painted many memorable images of both without ever including a recognizable landmark. In his art, the specificity of mood replaces the specificity of place. Another equally admired westerner, Richard Diebenkorn eventually abstained from even the pretense of landscape at all in his later Ocean Park abstract paintings, yet the essence of California light and color is retained in all its clarity in these works.

> "Sites disappear; others are created. That nasty little railroad station, devoid of taste and style, becomes an element of beauty in the landscape which at first it made ugly." Remy de Gourmont, *Promenades Philosophiques*, 1905[3]

Like Rene Magritte's famous paintings of darkened streets in lamplight combined with bright daytime skies, Aronson-Shore's depictions of the streets of Portsmouth and the hillsides of Monhegan Island are decidedly otherworldly—familiar yet foreign. Her distillation of place removes the flaws that are apparent in candid observation. The narrow streets of Strawbery Banke can actually be quite claustrophobic; the houses built far too close together and located so near the roads. The hardness of Monhegan Island, with houses clinging for dear life to the hillsides, is emblematic of a bleak existence for much of the year. The uniformly unadorned structures (in all these paintings), built for utility and longevity, can appear repetitious, devoid of individuality. However, through the brush of Aronson-Shore, these cramped streets and island crags become stage sets for the play of light and color. Her subtle rearrangement of foliage and buildings (her houses take on a variety of hues rather than the monotonous white that is all too common in New England) makes for tightly painted, crisply lit landscapes that demand attention.

Her individuality of artistic vision will be understood and appreciated by informed sensibilities but not by all. The very fact that she is a representational artist plying her trade in the year 2010 will be anathema to postmodernists who will react to her art like vampires to garlic. In turn, sentimentalists will yearn for more specificity of place, color, and light in her work to have her reassure through the replication of the familiar, which she is unwilling to do. Aronson-Shore follows her own creative path in transforming seemingly familiar places into an art of her own invention. These paintings represent the accumulated memory the artist has retained over time. They came more from observation than actual sketching or painting on site. She draws on those recollections like file cards of recognition that are reshuffled and rearranged as she sees fit in creating her stylized recreations of remembrance.

"A picture is something which requires as much knavery, trickery, and deceit as the perpetration of a crime. Paint falsely, and then add the accent of nature." Edgar Degas[4]

The light in Aronson-Shore's paintings is the calculated structure upon which her composition is built. Her deep blue and purple-tinged shadows define specific time—the long casts of shade could designate dawn or dusk. The light of early morning is usually thought of as soft and delicate, but the shadows of Aronson-Shore spill across her landscapes in an enveloping glow of gathering dusk. The sense of day's end and approaching night is the sensation that permeates these scenes despite their vibrant color. She consciously manipulates how light falls across her buildings and foliage to create a subtle but undeniably emotional basis for the viewer to experience. What adds to this mood is what is missing. The fact that no people are present to give animation and normalcy to these scenes makes their omission all the more poignant. Humanity is everywhere present through man-made structures yet no one is home in

*Spring Colors at Strawbery Banke*, oil on canvas, 16 x 20 in.

*Light and Shadow Rythms in Late Fall*, oil on canvas, 14 x 18 in.

Aronson-Shore's world. The accumulated sense of absence is emotionally reminiscent of the metaphysical landscapes of Giorgio de Chirico with his equally vacant Italian thoroughfares and piazzas. Whether the barren stretches of ocean in her Monhegan Island paintings or the empty streets of Portsmouth, Aronson-Shore's optimistic high-key tonalities interact with otherwise lonely locales.

In 1856, Camille Corot wrote, "Beauty in art is truth bathed in an impression from nature. I am struck upon seeing a certain place. While I strive for a conscientious imitation, I yet never for an instant lose the emotion that has taken hold of me. Reality is one part of art; feeling completes it... Before any site and any object, abandon yourself to your first impression. If you have really been touched, you will convey to others the sincerity of your emotion."[5] In these carefully constructed yet deeply felt reflections of New Hampshire and Maine, Carol Aronson-Shore has made us draw upon our own memories of place and experience. Even more, she has enveloped us in her highly personal world of color, form, and light.

Robert Flynn Johnson
Curator Emeritus, Achenbach Foundation for Graphic Arts
Fine Arts Museums of San Francisco

Notes
1. Peggy Hadden, ed., *The Quotable Artist* (New York: Allworth Press, 2007), 17.
2. Robert Goldwater and Marco Treves, Ed., *Artists on Art* (New York: Pantheon Books, 1947), 347–348.
3. Ian Crofton, ed., *A Dictionary of Art Quotations* (New York: Schirmer Books, 1989), 98.
4. Robert Goldwater and Marco Treves, ed., *Artists on Art* (New York: Pantheon Books, 1947), 308.
5. Ibid., 241.

*Blues and Reds Behind the Chase House*, oil on canvas, 30 x 30 in.

# THE STRAWBERY BANKE SERIES
## A Symphony in Seasonality

*Chase House Red Tree with Red Reflections*, gouache on paper, 7 x 7 in.

## Privileged Moments

*The museum village of Strawbery Banke has provided me with a wonderful, visual opportunity to explore my primary subject, which is the way color shapes pictorial light and space. In these paintings, color captures and defines the "privileged moments" during the day when light makes its appearance and disappearance, when shadows are at their longest and light is most clearly directional. These brief but special moments give expression to a world both at rest and in transition.[1]*

Carol Aronson-Shore

Still. Quiet. Frozen color. Sun rise or sunset; dawn or dusk; season by season. Whether the subject is a building still life wrapped in color or a biting, frozen landscape, Strawbery Banke Museum is captured repeatedly and painstakingly by Carol Aronson-Shore. As one who spends a great deal of time on the Strawbery Banke Museum campus, I am repeatedly struck by the manner in which Aronson-Shore captures light and mood with what appears to be such subtlety and unhurried ease. For example, *Blues and Reds Behind the Chase House* has an autumnal glow skillfully depicted in the window reflection at Rider-Wood House; red leaves carpet the grass under a twilight sky, and the majestic tree itself has a deep, almost velvety quality to it. Using classic techniques, the artist has foreshortened the perspective by using the distant house to terminate the view, leaving the visitor constrained on either side by visual roadblocks—left to behold the light making its appearance in the long shadows and to savor the tree's majesty. (For comparison, see *Chase House Red Tree with Red Reflections*, gouache on paper, 2010.)

The artist skillfully—almost surreptitiously—draws the observer into these dazzling color-drenched canvases. Upon arrival, however, Aronson-Shore has established the path she would like you to follow, based on careful application of terminal devices created by paths, fences, and individual building forms or walls of buildings. The experience is, in most cases, controlled even as specific objects in the landscape draw you closer—the red tree, the yellow house.

And yet one feels almost voyeuristic approaching the painting—sneaking inside and snooping around the canvas, wondering where are the people, the dogs, the breeze? It is in this privileged moment that one is struck by the dawn light creeping over the buildings, trees, and gardens, enveloping the world of Strawbery Banke in light; or, alternatively, the light is rapidly receding, soon to leave the campus in dark's stillness. What of the interloper? It is at that moment that the viewer feels the energy emanating from the power of nature. Color and light, light and form.

*Fresh Snowfall at the Peacock House*, oil on canvas, 14 x 18 in.

In Aronson-Shore's view *Morning Tree Shadows behind Yeaton-Walsh* (see page 18), the sun is rapidly ascending, creating a tantalizing shine on the pottery; the shadows indicate that the Strawbery Banke community will soon be enveloped by the sun. The viewer senses that it is the still quiet interstices found between dawn and sunrise. It is a moment shared between the canvas and the viewer. Motionless. There is no sense of rustling leaves (see *Red Tree at Chase House*, page 15), and even after a snowfall on the campus, all is calm, undisturbed. No animal tracks, human footfall, or snowmelt mars the purity of the moment as witnessed in paintings such as *Fresh Snowfall at the Peacock House* (2010). Only the shadows of the snowy tree limbs traverse the petrified scene.

Seasonality can be captured by snowfall or autumn leaves, but with Aronson-Shore that is almost unnecessary to understanding her work—the passage of the seasons is apparent through the raking light and shadows, voids and positives, tonal quality of color. Strong geometries anchor the compositions: note the bulkheads, chimneys, windows, and fences. Rigid building geometries and even the motionless trees have a sculpted rather than organic feel. Winter is captured and shaped by shadow and crisp, bright light.

When discussing *Fall Color at Strawbery Banke* (see page 21), the artist notes:

> [It] is a long, horizontal painting that literally presents itself as a scale balancing on one side the youthful red maple, proud and glorious in its peak fall color, against the severely pared-down geometry of the mustard-colored Rider-Wood House. This painting also balances the three

*Red Tree at the Chase House*, oil on canvas, 18 x 24 in.

*primary colors of red, yellow, and blue in almost full saturation. It is pictorially dramatic, setting the stage visually for a play of light, color, and contrasting forms.*[2]

Carol Aronson-Shore

The observer is presented with a perfect balance in time.

## The Continuum of Space and Time

The sense of timelessness is an appropriate theme for this seacoast community, which has developed over some four centuries. Strawbery Banke Museum is a ten-acre site in the heart of Portsmouth, New Hampshire, with historic structures ranging in date from 1695 forward and their corresponding historic gardens and landscapes.

Holding tremendous personal appeal to the author is Aronson-Shore's "village view" (*Early Morning Light at the End of Horse Lane*, see page 17). Here a path leads from just past Hough House to Sherburne House and across Puddle Dock to a tree and the split rail fence. This little-captured perspective of Strawbery Banke was first revealed to me by the artist. Aronson-Shore has at once managed to craft an image both contemporary and historic. The artist comments on this key aspect of her work:

*Created in the studio, the final landscapes have the quality of a stage elaborately set for human experience. They are once removed and stripped down as though seen through a selective filter. What emerges is a combination of both the specific reality of place and time along with the memory of a place suspended in time and detached.*[3]

Carol Aronson-Shore

*Long Shadows on the Lowd House*, gouache on paper, 6½ x 11⅜ in.

It is in this liminal state that Aronson-Shore achieves her strongest works.

One is prepared to be a more active participant (rather than a voyeur) in this scene, to meander down the dirt footpath. The site actually blocks out the city's current presence, through a variety of visual techniques. Aronson-Shore's painting looks toward the distant split

*Early Morning Light at the End of Horse Lane*, oil on canvas, 30 x 30 in.

*Morning Tree Shadows Behind the Yeaton-Walsh House*, oil on canvas, 30 x 30 in.

rail fence, but the parking lot, which terminates the view in reality, is not apparent. The slight grade of the path is included or assumed, simply by the shadows falling across it, and one feels prepared for a singular, solitary experience. Here, too, the well-known historic gardens of Strawbery Banke play an anchor role as do the voids created by green space.

Aronson-Shore's process of filtering or distillation is complex and intensely personal. Take for example her work in gouache on paper (*Long Shadows on Lowd House*, see page 16, or *Star Island Houses*, not pictured) as companions to her oils. The color palette is not as keyed up in these beautiful yet, by comparison, soft focus works. The medium does not lend itself to the severity of line and geometry found in the canvases with which we are now familiar. The experience for the viewer is not intermediated by the artist.

Among Aronson-Shore's many University of New Hampshire students, artist Molly Wensburg aptly reveals the importance of history and art in Aronson-Shore's teaching and, by extension, in her own work:

> As students, Carol made us feel as though we were connected to a larger artistic past, which extended far beyond the classroom, that we were part of an important artistic heritage shared with the artists of the past. More than any of my other instructors, Carol taught the importance and value of art history. She is so knowledgeable in this area.[4]

Molly Doe Wensberg

Aronson-Shore provides the perfect artistic rationale for the Strawbery Banke series when she elucidates, "I feel that this process of first working on site and later creating in the studio is essential to the subject of Strawbery Banke, the historic village that continues to evolve in time while it also evokes an earlier period."[5] The series offers new glimpses and original concepts to an environment steeped in history, creating fresh perspectives and innovative dialogues—held in balance by color, form, and light.

Kimberly Alexander, Ph.D.
Chief Curator, Strawbery Banke Museum

NOTES
1. Correspondence between Carol Aronson-Shore and the author, Friday, May 14, 2010.
2. Ibid.
3. Ibid.
4. Telephone interview with Molly Doe Wensberg and the author, Monday, June 28, 2010.
5. Op. cit.

*Snow Shadows and Shrubs Behind the Sherburne House*, oil on canvas, 18 x 24 in.

*Fall Color at Strawbery Banke*, oil on canvas, 24 x 42 in.

*Snow Behind the Goodwin Mansion*, oil on canvas, 16 x 20 in.

# VISIONS TRANSFORMED
## Recent Paintings by Carol Aronson-Shore

*We see in every work of figurative art the desire, objectively to represent beauty, solely through form and color, in mutually balanced relations, and, at the same time, an attempt to express that which these forms, colors, and relations arouse in us.*

Piet Mondrian, *Plastic Art and Pure Plastic Art*, 1937

A blank neutral surface. An array of pigments. These are the raw materials of any painting, whether abstract or figurative. The eternal mystery and magic, the seeming sleight of hand: how is it possible that so much can be communicated through such basic means? In the passage above, Mondrian attempted to make a case for "pure plastic art," which he believed to be superior to figurative art because it bypassed the subjectivity of the individual artist, and was thus more "universal." Later on in the same essay, he identified an important truth: that all nonfigurative art was drawn from the surrounding reality, and that all figurative art was based on "the dynamic rhythm of inherent formal relations."

Carol Aronson-Shore's latest series of paintings of Strawbery Banke in Portsmouth provides a wonderful example of the fundamentally abstract nature of figurative art. On the one hand, no one would mistake the works for nonreferential compositions of form, shapes, and color. They appear to be literal representations of actual places under specific conditions of light, and as such they are incontrovertibly "realistic," figurative paintings. Yet they are constructed through close attention to abstract principles of design and color, which the artist manipulates with incredible skill and deliberate control. Paradoxically, these abstract elements are the means through which Aronson-Shore suggests a vivid, palpable, glowing, evocation of the real world.

Starting from the details of the particular, the artist pursues her lifelong passion for finding the visual vehicle for depicting the interrelationship of structure, color, and light. In so doing, she breaks from what she describes as the "tyranny of the real" to create tightly constructed, finely tuned, dynamic symphonies of color. The title of the exhibit, *The Shape of Color*, reflects Aronson-Shore's commitment to the primacy of the formal aspects of her work. But in contrast to Mondrian's assertion that in figurative art, subject matter, i.e., the "personal," gets in the way of effective visual communication, in Aronson-Shore's work the buildings of Strawbery Banke seen in the early morning or late afternoon light, with all their many levels of individual and cultural associations, resonate with a depth of meaning that communicates not only in formal terms, but also in relation to the experience of being human on this earth.

## Seeing into Painting

Aronson-Shore begins her paintings by working on site, encountering a particular landscape under certain conditions, and sketching and making smaller paintings of what she sees. She describes the experience of being in the landscape in a receptive mode as having "an immense power and concreteness over [her] imagination." She then returns to the studio where she distills her visual experiences into canvases that, while they embody her actual experience, vary many of the literal elements in order to more effectively express her visual and emotional response to the landscape. The method of taking copious visual notes in plein air, and composing them into final paintings in the studio, is one used by many landscape painters since the early nineteenth century. John Constable, for example, made numerous rough sketches and paintings that he took back to his studio where he first created full-scale painted studies before he ultimately executed his finished canvases. Similarly, Aronson-Shore creates smaller-scale and more rapidly painted works in gouache that she often turns into her final larger paintings in oil.

According to the artist, in all of her works, a primary step is to "tie the representation to the picture plane as well as [to] suggest modifications to the observed forms based on the pictorial needs of the format chosen." In other words, her task is to distill her experience of the actual landscape into a dynamic two-dimensional form, which she achieves by creating a tight, cohesive, logical, well-balanced pictorial structure. As she says, "discovering and revealing the underlying structural elements are one of my primary preoccupations and in many ways, my real subject."

## The Constructed Landscape

Aronson-Shore skillfully controls and modulates the viewer's entrance into the space of representation. In several paintings, a large dark form dominates the left-hand side of the picture surface and leads us into the work by serving as a framing element much as a curtain around a stage both focuses the viewer's attention on the unfolding scene and demarcates the boundary between the actual and theatrical space. Consistent with this technique, Aronson-Shore says

*Late Light Panorama in Fall*, oil on canvas, 24 x 42 in.

that her "final landscapes have the quality of a stage or movie set for human experience."

In *Snow Behind the Goodwin Mansion*, we are led into the space of the painting by the L shape formed by the dark vertical wall of the most proximate structure, which covers most of the left-hand border, and by the deep bluish horizontal band of snow that stretches the length of the work's bottom edge, on which the dark wall rests. Together, these constitute a frame, a device used to delineate the break between the real world and the world of illusion. She uses a similar approach in *Morning Tree Shadows Behind the Yeaton-Walsh House* (see page 18), in which the implied L of the frame created by the building wall on the left-hand border and dark green grass on the bottom edge takes up a larger area of the canvas to focus the viewer's attention on the orange tree glowing in the distance.

Aronson-Shore moves the viewer around the pictorial space through the repetition of geometrical forms, which through their mutual resonance also serve to unify the picture surface. In *Snow Behind the Goodwin Mansion* (see page 22), the slanting rooflines of the two houses in the mid-ground form a dynamic triangle that is echoed by the implied outline of the large pine on the left. The L shape formed at the left-hand corner is repeated in the middle ground by the right-hand edge of the ochre house and a fence. The calligraphic natural lines of the trees on both sides are mediated by the linear shadows on the snow-covered roof. In *Blues and Reds Behind the Chase House* (see page 12), there is a dramatic triangle formed in the mid-ground between the slanted roof of a white house on the left and a brilliant red tree on the right. This form intersects with three other triangles created by the outline of the trees on the right and the progression through space of the houses on the left.

Aronson-Shore also uses the interplay of the built environment's geometric shapes and the organic shapes of the natural world around them to modulate the viewer's movement through pictorial space. In *Blues and Reds Behind the Chase House*, natural forms predominate on the right side, while the man-made are mostly on the left. In *Snow Behind the Goodwin Mansion*, layers of buildings and trees are intercalated, with the wall in the foreground and the ochre house in the mid-ground separated by a large snow-laden pine. In *Late Light Panorama in Fall* (see page 25), the viewer moves deeply into the space of the canvas, from left to right through a layered succession of houses and trees whose trajectory is consistent with the slanted light of late autumn.

## Color and Light

Color is at the heart of Aronson-Shore's paintings. She has said that color shapes her work, that experiences of color are its real subject, and that expressive color is what motivates her to

*Yellow House at Strawbery Banke*, oil on canvas, 14 x 18 in.
Private collection.

*Museum Hill and Bell,* oil on canvas, 20 x 24 in.

paint. The work, itself, communicates the artist's strong feelings about color and its importance to her artistic endeavor. Simply put, Aronson-Shore's paintings appear to glow, almost as if they emanated their own light. This effect of light-suffused color is achieved through extremely careful and skilled manipulation.

She creates a color harmony through a limited palette in which the complementary colors purple and gold predominate in *Snow Behind the Goodwin Mansion*. These hues are picked up throughout the image to unify the picture surface and keep the viewer's eye active: the purple in the low lights of the snow on the large pine tree that separates them, in the branches of the tree that extend into the right-hand border, in the windows of the house behind those branches, and even in the lower right-hand corner. The gold is used more sparingly and is concentrated in the depiction of the house, a thin line below it, subtle highlights in the fence, and chimney.

Aronson-Shore is not afraid to use highly saturated colors, placed strategically, to create vivid contrasts, as in *Yellow House at Strawbery Banke* (see page 27), which is imbued with the almost otherworldly glow of late afternoon autumnal light. An orange tree blazes out against a deep blue sky, its brightness further emphasized by the gray produced through the subdued greens (a bush form) and reds (a house) to its left. Likewise, a tree of a slightly darker orange hue glows against the face of a house whose salmon color contains streaks of purple. And the side of the yellow house itself is incandescent in contrast to the front, which has been toned down to ochre, and to the lavender roof and windows. Aronson-Shore speaks of finding conversations between colors, in which "a red speaks to a certain kind of blue and a third color emerges. A yellow turns from warm to cool and creates a feeling of light shifting and moving around us."

*Monhegan Island Village Views*, gouache on paper, 6 x 6 in.

## Position in Her Oeuvre

Aronson-Shore has said that the Strawbery Banke paintings grew out of her previous series focusing on Monhegan Island, some of which are included in the current exhibition. It was on Monhegan Island that she was particularly struck by the contrast between human-made forms and

*Wyeth House at Dusk II*, oil on canvas, 20 x 24 in.

the natural world they inhabit, as seen under specific light conditions. She saw the "stark relationship of architecture and landscape as a metaphor for the individual." In *Wyeth House at Dusk, II* (see page 30), for example, the house is perched at the juncture of land, sea, and sky and in the artist's words, "commands the landscape elements like an orchestral conductor." The sky in this work is especially dramatic, and like others in the Monhegan series such as *Approaching Manana Island* and *Museum Window at Dusk* (see page 28), the work appears to radiate an internal light source.

*Approaching Manana Island*, oil on canvas, 18 x 24 in.

Both the Monhegan and Strawbery Banke series consolidate and extend pictorial concerns that Aronson-Shore explored in her earlier work. That glowing light, itself, characterizes all her landscape series whatever their focus: the tropics, Italy, or New England. She has long been interested in exploring abstract structures and framing devices, in her early circus works where figures are caught in linear nets and in her 1990s series of altarpieces where she uses an external structure. In *Icon for the Musical Ratios of Nature* (not pictured), she experimented with the use of a gold-leaf frame to pick up the scintillating light in the image. The works in this series are the culmination of a lifetime of looking and painting.

## Existential Light

*Museum Window at Dusk*, oil on canvas, 20 x 24 in.

Musing on Edward Hopper's famous yet overly simplified statement that all he was trying to do was to paint light on a wall, Aronson-Shore concludes that "the light he painted on the wall captured everything—mood, time, space, the feel of the air, a distant memory of an experience." Hopper's paintings had an important early impact on Aronson-Shore, and this description of the existential potential of Hopper's depiction of light applies to her own works, as well as providing a key toward understanding their expressive content.

Strawbery Banke is a very evocative setting because it is a memento from the past that exists in the present. The buildings and their layout are remnants of a previous age, from which

*Dock Houses and Manana*, oil on canvas, 20 x 24 in.

the earthly indwellers of the past call to us across time, sending messages through their built environment. Because it is an actual setting, it has tangibility and presence; it both encompasses us and interacts with the natural world contained within it. Additionally, fragments of this pristinely preserved space echo in our consciousness when we walk through Portsmouth streets or drive through the New England countryside.

Aronson-Shore chooses to depict Strawbery Banke at what she calls "privileged" moments—early morning, late afternoon—when the shadows are long and the light is glowing and transformative. These are liminal times that mark the transition from night to day and day to night, and as such they are magical. This light touches something very profound within each of us and, along with the past's echo and the interplay of natural and human-made forms, arouses both memory and desire.

*Monehgan Island Red Roof Looking to Sea*, gouache on paper, 6 x 6 in.

It is especially fitting, then, that the images themselves are painted from memory. They begin with an actual encounter—sharp angles of crystalline light seen on a cold winter morning, the long tongues of shadows lapping at the fading light of an autumn day. But they are distillations of that experience into something more universal: line, shape, color, geometry. Like the poet William Wordsworth's daffodils, they are born of "emotion recollected in tranquility," seen with the "inward eye" and wrought anew with paint upon canvas.

Mara Witzling, Ph.D.
Professor, Art and Art History
University of New Hampshire

*Harbor Boats*, oil on canvas, 16 x 20 in.

*Beach View of Island Inn*, oil on canvas, 16 x 20 in.

# INDEX